Firefighters
to the Rescue
Around the World

Linda Staniford

raintree

Raintree is an imprint of Capstone Global Library Limited, a company incorporated in England and Wales having its registered office at 7 Pilgrim Street, London, EC4V 6LB – Registered company number: 6695582

www.raintree.co.uk
myorders@raintree.co.uk

Edited by Linda Staniford
Designed by Steve Mead
Picture research by Eric Gohl
Production by Victoria Fitzgerald
Originated by Capstone Global Library Ltd
Printed and bound in China

ISBN 978 1 474 71523 2 (hardback)
19 18 17 16 15
10 9 8 7 6 5 4 3 2 1

ISBN 978 1 474 71532 4 (paperback)
20 19 18 17 16
10 9 8 7 6 5 4 3 2 1

British Library Cataloguing in Publication Data
A full catalogue record for this book is available from the British Library.

Acknowledgements
We would like to thank the following for permission to reproduce photographs:
Alamy: Ace Stock Limited, 7, Ian Marlow, 13, 22 (top), John Joannides, 20, Mia Caruana, 6; AP Photo: The Yomiuri Shimbun, 5; Getty Images: Christopher Furlong, 19, Corpo Nazionale dei Vigili del Fuoco, 17, Orlando Sierra, 18, Stringer/STR, 15; iStockphoto: erlucho, 10, Graffizone, back cover (right), 12, omgimages, 21, slobo, back cover (left), 8; Newscom: Broker/olf image, 9, 22 (middle), Xinhua News Agency/Country Fire Authority, 14, 22 (bottom), Xinhua News Agency/Zhang Jia, 11; Shutterstock: art-pho, cover (bottom), Jerry Sharp, 4, Ververidis Vasilis, cover (top); U.S. Coast Guard: 16

Design Elements: Shutterstock

Contents

Some words are shown in bold, **like this**. You can find out what they mean by looking in the glossary.

How do firefighters help us?

Firefighters are always ready to rush to the rescue. When a fire starts they work hard to put it out as quickly as they can.

Firefighters also deal with other kinds of emergencies all over the world. For example, they rescue people trapped in cars or in floods.

What do firefighters wear?

A firefighter wears a **waterproof** jacket and boots. They are made of **fireproof** material that will not melt in the heat of a fire.

Firefighters also wear helmets to protect their heads. The helmet has a **visor**. It protects the firefighter's face from the heat.

How do firefighters travel?

A fire engine carries firefighters and their equipment to a burning building. Fire engines are brightly coloured. They have a flashing light and a loud **siren**.

In Venice, Italy, people travel on **canals** instead of roads, so firefighters use boats to get to fires. Some firefighters use motorcycles to reach fires quickly.

What equipment do firefighters have?

Fire engines carry some water in tanks, but they also have very long hoses. These can be connected to fire **hydrants** to pump water onto the fire.

hydrant

Fire engines also have long ladders on the roof. Firefighters use these to climb up high buildings to rescue people from inside the buildings.

What else do firefighters carry?

Axes and rams are used to get into locked buildings to rescue people. Fire **extinguishers** help put out special kinds of fires, such as electrical fires.

After a traffic accident, firefighters help rescue people trapped in their cars. They use gas torches to cut the metal.

What types of fire are there?

In Australia, it can be very hot and dry.
Bush fires can spread very quickly.
Firefighters use helicopters to spray water
on to the fire to control it.

Special teams of firefighters deal with fires at airports. Planes carry a lot of fuel, which can burn very quickly if it catches fire.

How do firefighters save lives at sea?

Oil rig fires are very **dangerous** because all the oil nearby keeps them burning. Firefighters on boats spray sea water at the fires for a long time to put them out.

Firefighters can rescue people who are trapped on a boat that is sinking. They have special equipment to cut through the side of the boat so they can bring the trapped people out to safety.

How else do firefighters rescue people?

When there is an earthquake, buildings may **collapse**. Firefighters can rescue people who are trapped underneath the **rubble**.

When there is a flood, people may get trapped upstairs in their houses or on the roof. Firefighters use boats to get to them and take them to dry land.

Making the world a safer place!

Firefighters often visit schools and communities. They show people what to do if something catches fire in their home.

Firefighters are very brave people. It is good to know we can call them if there is a fire. But it is also important to know how to stay safe near fires.

Quiz

What have you learned about firefighters around the world?

Question 1

What are gas torches used for?
a) to give light
b) to put out fires
c) to cut metal so that people trapped inside cars can be rescued

Question 2

What kind of transport do firefighters use in Venice?
a) boats
b) motor cycles
c) bicycles

Question 3

How do firefighters put out bush fires in Australia?
a) using fire extinguishers
b) by spraying water from helicopters
c) by climbing ladders

Answers: 1 c), 2 a), 3 b)

Glossary

bush fire fire in the countryside where the grass and bushes burn very fast

canal human-made waterway

collapse fall down suddenly; buildings often collapse during earthquakes

dangerous likely to cause harm or injury

extinguisher a device with water and chemicals inside it that is used to put out fires

fireproof does not burn

hydrant a large, upright pipe with a valve that draws water from the city's water supply. Hydrants supply water for fighting fires.

rubble broken bricks and other material left from a building that has fallen down or been demolished

siren a device that makes a loud sound

visor a covering, often attached to a hat or helmet, designed to shade the eyes

waterproof able to keep water out

Find out more

Books

Diary of a Firefighter, Angela Royston (Raintree, 2013)
Firefighter: People who Help Us, Rebecca Hunter (Tulip Books, 2014)
First Book of Emergency Vehicles, Isabel Thomas (A&C Black, 2014)
When I Grow Up: Firefighter, Clare Hibbert (Ladybird, 2015)

Websites

Find out more about firefighters at these sites:

http://www.explainthatstuff.com/firefighting.html
http://www.factmonster.com/ipka/A0934701.html

Index